S. R Gridley, W Barnes

Bristol Jersey Herd Book

Comprising Cattle Bred in Bristol

S. R Gridley, W Barnes

Bristol Jersey Herd Book
Comprising Cattle Bred in Bristol

ISBN/EAN: 9783337408497

Printed in Europe, USA, Canada, Australia, Japan

Cover: Foto ©ninafisch / pixelio.de

More available books at **www.hansebooks.com**

BRISTOL

JERSEY HERD BOOK,

COMPRISING,

CATTLE BRED IN BRISTOL, CONN.,

AND ITS VICINITY,

WITH THEIR ANTECEDENTS AND DESCENDENTS.

ARRANGED BY

S. R. GRIDLEY and W. BARNES.

MARCH, 1869.

———— ◆ ————

HARTFORD:
PRESS OF WILEY, WATERMAN & EATON.
1869.

PREFACE.

The primary object of this book was to trace out Jersey Stock owned, at different times, by ourselves, back to importation. But it very soon became apparent that in breeding, buying, and selling Jerseys, for the last twelve years, the blood of the original Stock, introduced into our town, had been widely disseminated.

The purpose was then formed to include all Jerseys owned in Bristol up to the early part of 1869. It is believed that every full blooded Jersey, that ever stood in this town, is recorded in this book, and the offspring of every pure bred female, whether from pure bred Bulls or otherwise; the authorities being quoted in fine print preceding each number.

In arranging the within Pedigrees, we have endeavored to render them simple and exact. In a few instances the latter has been impossible, and we have been obliged to be content with tracing the Pedigrees to the herds of well known breeders, having their assurance that the animals in question were thorough bred Jerseys.

Many breeders who have taken great pains, and have been to great expense to keep their herds, have not been careful to keep accurate records of the Pedigrees of their Stock, feeling that as long as they themselves were satisfied, their assurance would be sufficient to convince purchasers.

This course answered, when there was but few Cattle of this breed in the country, and the necessity of an organized effort to preserve the purity of the blood had not been recognized. But the time has now come when Pedigrees are expected with each thorough bred animal.

The increased demand for these justly celebrated Butter Cows has, in too many instances, thrown *impure* animals upon the markets. Hence the necessity of a Herd Book.

We have been placed under renewed obligations to some gentlemen who have kindly given us information, by mail, respecting their animals, saving us much time in the compilation of this work. To those who have withheld information, when requested to give it, making this book imperfect in some respect, we can only regret that they have given so little attention to breeding, and created suspicion on the part of their animals.

With the hope that, in *future*, every breeder will name each animal with an original name on the day of its birth, and keep a full record of all animals, and by so doing dispose of all question as to purity of blood; this work is respectfully submitted by the Authors.

INDEX OF ANIMALS.

Accidental,	45
Adventure, . .	87
Alloy, . . .	57
Amy, . .	145
April Fool, .	32
Angeline, . .	31
Angelina Baker, .	21
Baltimore, .	94
Baptist, . . .	12
Bashan, .	102
Beauty, . . .	126
Belle,	45
Belle Isle, . . .	50
Bergamot, .	61
Bess, . . .	122
Blanche, .	7, 85
Blade, . .	35
Bill, . .	28, 101
Bismarck, . . .	118
Blossom, . .	57
Brickbat, . . .	88
Brenda,	135
Bristol, . .	66
Brice, . .	23
Buck, Daniel, . .	10
Burdell, .	107
Butter Cup, . .	134
Butter Cup, 2d, .	110
Butter Cup, 3d, . .	111
Cactus, . . .	33
Cæsar, .	89
Camelia, .	32
Challenger, . .	84

Charles, .	110
Chamoise, .	51
Cherry,	15
Clifton, .	98
Climax, . . .	104
Clover, . . 8, 27, 89, 120
Clover, 2d, . .	17
Colonel, . . . 80, 114
Commodore Nutt, .	15
Commodore, . .	76
Comet, 24, 116
Competitor,	85
Connecticut, .	33
Corporal, .	17
Cowslip,	28
Creampot, .	90
Crocus, .	24
Dahlia, . . .	93
Daisy, . . 1, 13, 20, 34, 87
Daisy, . . 99, 123, 137
Daisy, 2d, . .	125
Dan, .	96
Dan Buck, Jr.,	11
Delight, .	39
Dew Drop,	75
Diaz, .	37
Dick, .	100
Dick Swiveller,	112
Disappointment, . .	35
Dolly, . . 19, 96
Dolly, 2d, .	97
Duke, . . 60, 81
Dust, . . .	92
Duchess, . . .	136

Effie, . . .	60	Jenny, . .	2
Emily, .	86	Jerry, .	82
Emperor, . .	6	Jessamine, .	. 114
Emperor, 2d, .	. 7	Jessie, . .	131
Eureka, . .	105	Jersey, . .	1, 108
Experiment, . .	46	Jersey, 2d, . .	2
		Jersey, 5th,	. 3
Fanny, . .	67	Jonathan, . . .	61
Fanny Fawn, .	70	John, . . .	. 56
Fate, . . .	74	Joe Hooker, .	49
Fawn, . . .	5, 37	Juda, . . .	. 138
Fawnett, .	71	June, .	23
Flirt, . .	6, 41	Juno, .	42
Fern, . .	54	Julian, . . .	91
Flora, . . 30, 95, 125		Jupiter, .	. 75
Flora, 2d, . . .	94		
Fortune, .	27	Kid, . . .	47
Frank, . .	55	Kitty, . . .	14, 38
Freedom, . .	109		
		Lady Alderney, .	84
Gone, . .	31	Lady Ashley, . .	139
Grace, .	82	Lady Alice, . .	. 66
Grade, . .	29	Lady Clarence, . .	144
General Grant,	30	Lady Martin, . .	. 140
Gray Eagle,	68	Lady Messervy, . .	143
Gray Eagle, 2d,	. 72	Lady Montague, .	. 142
		Lady Stanley, . .	106
Halicarnassus, . .	34	Lantanna, . .	. 77
Halo, . .	48	Leah, . . .	132
Harwinton, .	93	Lillie, . 73, 81, 102, 105, 108	
Hellen, . .	. 53	Little Fanny, . .	69
Hellen Dunbar, .	119	Little Fawn, .	. 68
Hemlock, .	73	Living Storm, .	26
Henry N., .	13	Lizzie, .	49
Hicks, .	9	Lost, . .	78
Highhorn,	127	Lola Montez, .	. 141
Hugo, .	18	Lucelle, .	80
Inez, .	59		
Irene, .	63	Magnolia, .	. 44
		Major, . .	. 79, 113
Jane,	52	Mars, . .	. 59
Jack, .	16, 39	Martha, .	88
Janett, . . .	56	Marigold, . .	. 65

Mattie,	79	Sam,	64, 90
McClellan,	25	Shambles,	53
Merrit,	58	Simmer,	69
Meekness,	76	Snowberry,	20
Mignionette,	11	Snowdrop,	47
Mingo,	41	Snow Flakes,	9, 16
Minnie,	83	Splendid,	4
Miss Take,	46	Splendid, Jr.,	95
		Spot,	52
Napoleon,	115	Stafford,	51
Narragausett,	86	Star,	77
Nellie,	58, 62, 98	Stillman,	71
Nellie, 1st,	115	Sue,	26
Nellie, 2d,	64, 116	Suky,	36
Nellie, 3d,	117	Surprise,	43
Newtown,	65	Susie,	40
Non Est,	29		
		Tabby,	10
Oakland,	99	Tanner,	70
		Tanner Cow,	112
Pale Nose,	128	Tanner Heifer,	113
Pansy,	22, 72, 100	Taurus,	14
Pete,	62	Tempest,	12
Pequabuck,	83	Tommy,	97
Phil Sheridan,	43	Tom Thumb,	36
Phœbe,	91	Topsey,	48
Plade,	18	Tulip,	118, 124
Polly,	104		
Prince,	8, 106	Ulysses,	92
Prince, 2d,	42	Uncas,	103
Prize,	109		
		Victor,	50
Rachael,	133	Violet,	25, 103
Raghorn,	5		
Reindeer,	22	Waterbury,	21
Repent,	40	Whit,	63
Reverse,	38	White Oak,	74
Role,	44	Wide Awake,	19
Romeo,	54	Winonia,	4
Rosalie,	55		
Rose,	3, 78, 107	Xiphias,	111
Rose Bud,	129		
Rose Leaf,	130	Young Roger,	67
Rosy,	101	Yok,	117

JERSEY POINTS.

1. Small head; tapering to a black nose; with broad, mealy muzzle.
2. Level or dish face; large placid eye; quirl low down.
3. Small horn, amber color, tipped with black.
4. Long, thin ear; orange color within.
5. THIN NECK and CLEAR THROAT.
6. Thin withers; sloping shoulders.
7. Level back to setting on of tail.
8. Hips good breadth; long from point to end of haunch bone.
9. Deep flank, showing rear capacity of barrel; fore parts wedge shape.
10. Level fore bag; large milk veins, and long.
11. Hind bag full, and well up behind.
12. Strong milk mirror; good escutcheon, indicating duration of milk.
13. MEDIUM SIZED TEATS, SQUARELY SET.
14. Small tail, long and slim.
15. Small legs.
16. Hoof amber color, or black.
17. Fine, soft hair; loose hide.
18. Nearly solid colors.—Seventeen and a half lbs. of butter per week.

INDEX OF OWNERS.

Allen, R. D. H.—Bull, 92. Cows, 71, 99.
Andrews, R. M.—B. 44, 45.
Atkins, Avery.—B. 33, 54. C. 64.
Atwood, A. L.—B. 51.
Austin, J. H.—B. 18. C. 14.

Baldwin, N. T.—B. 111. C. 87.
Ball, Amzi.—B. 69.
Bartholomew, Asa.—C. 138.
Barnes, Thomas.—B. 15, 52, 69, 78. C. 11, 84, 85, 86, 87, 92.
Barnes, Wallace.—B. 3, 7, 15, 26, 33, 35, 37, 53, 60, 61, 62, 65, 66, 67, 68,
    99, 111, 117, 118. C. 3, 6, 15, 17, 28, 30, 31, 32, 33, 35,
    36, 40, 44, 47, 50, 51, 54, 61, 62, 63, 65, 66, 67, 73, 74,
    75, 76, 79, 81, 82, 83, 84, 85, 87, 93, 143, 144, 145.
Beach, Burr S.—B. 91. C. 97, 139.
Bassett, H. W.—B. 104.
Bidwell, N. L.—C. 111, 114.
Bird, Jonathan.—B. 6, 7. C. 4, 5.
Bradley, John R.—B. 93.
Bradley, A. A.—C. 26, 96, 103.
Brown, William.—B. 5, 12, 21.
Brown, J. Carter.—B. 84. C. 131.
Buck, Daniel.—B. 10, 14, 19, 20, 21. C. 10, 17, 28, 39, 86, 96, 104, 108.
Bull, William.—B. 22, 41. C. 17, 37, 51, 132, 133.

Cairns, Robert.—B. 54.
Cameron, R. W.—B. 98.
Carrington, S. H.—B. 14.
Churchill, C.—B. 7.
Clarendon, Thos.—C. 90.
Collins, David.—B. 3. C. 96.
Colt, Elisha.—B. 27, 102. C. 25, 123, 124, 127.
Colt, Roswell, L.—B. 19, 24. C. 21, 134.
Colt, Col. Samuel.—B. 101. C. 120.

2

Corning, Erastus.—C. 88.
Cowles, Egbert.—B. 97, 105. C. 27, 29, 126, 127, 128.
Cowles, F. W.—C. 123, 125.
Cushing, Mr.—B. 79, 80.

Day, H. E.—B. 108. C. 134.
Dana, David.—C. 136.
Dodge, H. B.—B. 36, 37, 38. C. 36, 41, 42, 54.
Dunbar, E. L.—B. 5, 12, 17, 21, 29, 30, 31, 34, 46, 47, 48, 51, 55, 56, 57,
    58, 65, 66, 97, 110. C. 6, 14, 15, 26, 27, 29, 44, 52, 53,
    61, 64, 66, 68, 69, 70, 71, 116.
Dunham, Austin.—C. 25.

Eaton, Edward O.—C. 30, 73, 85.

Giles, John.—B. 96.
Goddard, Wm.—B. 84, 85, 86, 104. C. 94, 95, 131.
Goldsborough, Martin.—C. 7, 81, 82, 83.
Gomme, John T.—C. 14, 31, 33, 50, 54.
Gridley, George.—B. 97. C. 123.
Gridley, S. R.—B. 5, 7, 9, 11, 12, 13, 22, 27, 28, 39, 93, 94. C. 3, 6, 9,
    10, 12, 17, 18, 19, 20, 23, 24, 27, 28, 36, 38, 39, 43, 103,
    104, 123, 140, 141, 142.
Guild, Wm. A.—B. 82, 83. C. 93.

Hadsell, Geo. I.—B. 37.
Hale, Frank.—B. 67.
Hart, Isaac P.—C. 118.
Hart, S. N.—B. 83. C. 19.
Hart, Sylvester.—B. 32.
Henshaw, Mr.—C. 16.
Hitchcock, Geo. C.—B. 67. C. 19, 20, 47.
Hollister, L. H.—B. 46, 57. C. 29.
Hudson, M.—C. 108, 109, 124.
Hudson, P. W.—B. 98, 99, 100, 103. C. 28, 120.
Hungerford, W. M.—B. 5. C. 1, 3.

Judson, Russell.—B. 59, 76. C. 52, 70, 85.

Kent, H. H.—C. 121.
Kilbourn, F. J.—B. 72.

Leavett, David, Jr.—B. 34.
Lewis, Gad.—B. 27.

Lewis, George.—C. 105, 106.
Lewis, Wm.—C. 29.
Lonsdale Company.—B. 84, 104. C. 122.

Mackie, J. Milton.—C. 73.
Martin, O. Ives.—B. 30.
Massachusetts Ag. Society.—C. 91.
Motley, Thomas.—B. 81, 112, 113, 114. C. 135.
Merrick, A. N.—B. 61. C. 40.
Merrills, John L.—B. 28, 41.
Mills, Lyman A.—C. 117, 119.

Newell, S. D.—C. 109.
North, O. B.—C. 81.
Northrop, George.—B. 65.
Norton, Charles.—C. 127, 128.
Norton. Edgar A.—B. 43, 107. C. 45, 47, 51.
Norton, John T.—B. 1, 2, 3, 4, 26. C. 1, 2, 22.

Page, Mr.—C. 112.
Pattee, James.—C. 129, 130.
Peck, Henry.—B. 88, 90.
Pond, C. M.—C. 117.
Powell, J. B.—C. 41.

Redmond, William.—B. 23, 25.
Reed, E. M.—B. 80, 116.
Reed, Ransom.—C. 138.
Rhodes, Frank.—B. 95.
Riggs, Doct. J. M.—C. 52.
Robbins, S. W.—B. 19, 26. C 8.
Rockwell, J. T.—B. 68, 70, 71, 72, 73, 74, 75, 109, 111. C. 84, 88, 89, 90.
Russ, Addison.—B. 43, 64. C. 34, 77, 78, 80, 126.
Russell, Henry E.—B. 96.

Shelden, James O.—C. 6, 15, 32, 61, 63, 65, 66, 77.
Sherwood, S. S.—C. 26.
Smith, William H.—B. 8, 16, 42, 49, 50, 77. C. 13, 44, 48, 49.
Stanley, Henry.—C. 106.
Stevens, Parian.—C. 137.
Sutliff, John H.—B. 8, 16, 42, 76, 77, 78, 87, 88, 89, 90, 91, 92, 110. C.
        7, 55, 77, 96, 97, 98, 99, 100, 101, 102.

Taintor, John A.—B. 4, 8, 11, 19, 34, 51, 65, 106. C. 1, 2, 7, 8, 11, 16,
           22, 25, 26, 27, 37, 61, 67, 68, 74, 75, 81, 84, 105, 107,
           110, 112, 115.
Tanner, Warner.—C. 113, 115.
Tuttle, Luther.—B. 87.

Warner, Merritt.—B. 40. C. 45, 46, 50.
Waters, Joseph M.—B. 36. C. 41.
Webster, Hon. Daniel.—C. 121.
Whittemore, A. J.—B. 15, 35, 63. C. 43.
Wilcox, M. E.—B. 60. C. 24, 111, 114, 125.
Williams, Jas. B.—C. 28.
Wright, F. L.—B. 21, 32. C. 31, 32, 33, 34.

Yeomans, Wm. H.—B. 103. C. 116, 117, 118, 119.

BULLS.

J. T. NORTON.   ## 1 Jersey 1st,

Imported in the Cow DAISY (No. 1) August, 1852; owned by JOHN T. NORTON.

J. T. N.   ## 2 Jersey 2d,

Sire JERSEY 1st (No. 1); Dam DAISY (No. 1); was owned by JOHN T. NORTON.

J. T. N.   ## 3 Jersey 5th,

Sire JERSEY 2d (No. 2); Dam JENNY (No. 2); birth Sept. 21st, 1854; bred by JOHN T. NORTON; sold to WALLACE BARNES, May 28th, 1855; sold to DAVID COLLINS, Avon, Ct.

J. T. N.   ## 4 Splendid,

COLOR YELLOW.

Imported from Island of Jersey by JOHN A. TAINTOR, for JOHN T. NORTON, on brig Splendid, from Havre, and landed May 20th, 1856; slaughtered by Mr. NORTON in January, 1861.

S. R. G.   ## 5 Raghorn,

Sire SPLENDID (No. 4); Dam Rose (No. 3); birth April 27th, 1859; color yellow; bred by W. M. HUNGERFORD; sold by S. R. GRIDLEY, to E. L. DUNBAR, Bristol, Ct.; sold by DUNBAR, to WM. BROWN, Waterbury, Ct.; slaughtered by him.

T. M. STOUGHTON. 6 **Emperor,**

Imported by JONATHAN BIRD, of Belvidere, N. J., from Island of Jersey.

T. M. S.—S. R. G. 7 **Emperor 2d,**

Sire EMPEROR (No. 6); Dam FAWN, otherwise NEOCOMIS (No. 5); bred by JONATHAN BIRD; bought by S. R. GRIDLEY, Dec. 23d, 1858, of Mr. BIRD's agent, T. M. STOUGHTON, Greenfield, Mass.; slaughtered by CHAS. CHURCHILL, in 1861-2.

J. H. S. 8 **Prince,**

Sire SPLENDID (4); Dam Blanche (7); birth October 23d, 1859; bred by JOHN A. TAINTOR; sold by JOHN H. SUTLIFF to Dr. WM. H. SMITH, Newport, R. I., in 1863.

B. R. G. 9 **Hicks,**

Sire EMPEROR 2d (7); Dam ROSE (3); birth February 10th, 1861; bred by S. R. GRIDLEY.

S. R. G. **10,**

DANIEL BUCK's old Bull in 1856.

J. A. T.—S. R. G. 11 **Dan Buck, Jr.,**

Sire ——— (10); Dam CLOVER (8); bought by S. R. GRIDLEY of J. A. TAINTOR, in 1858.

S. R. G. 12 **Tempest,**

Sire JACK (16); Dam ROSE (3); birth March 28th, 1864; bred by S. R. GRIDLEY; sold E. L. DUNBAR, July 8th, 1864, and by him to WM. BROWN.

S. R. G. 13 **Henry N.,**

Sire COMMODORE NUTT (15); Dam ROSE (3); birth March, 1865; bred by S. R. GRIDLEY; died a calf.

S. H. C. **14 Taurus,**

Sire DANIEL BUCK's Bull; Dam, D. BUCK's large old Cow; birth 1853; black and white; bought of DANIEL BUCK by SILAS H. CARRINGTON; died Mr. CARRINGTON's in 1855, having served no full blood Cows.

T. B.—W. B. **15 Commodore Nutt,**

Sire EMPEROR 2d (7); Dam MIGNIONETEE (11); birth April, 1861; color, yellow; bred by THOMAS BARNES, Bristol, Conn.; bought by W. BARNES of Dr. A. J. WHITTEMORE, in April, 1863; castrated in 1865.

J. H. S. **16 Jack,**

Sire RAGHORN (5); Dam DAISY (13); birth August 19th, 1862; bred by JOHN H. SUTLIFF; sold Dr. WM. H. SMITH, Newport, R. I., 1863.

E. L. D. **17 Corporal,**

Sire COMMODORE NUTT 15; Dam KITTY 14; birth March, 1865; bred by E. L. DUNBAR; deaconed.

J. H. A. **18 Hugo,**

Sire WATERBURY (21); Dam KITTY 14; slaughtered a calf, by J. H. AUSTIN, in 1866.

J. A. T.—(P. W. HUDSON.) **19 Wide Awake,**

Imported in a Cow by ROSWELL L. COLT, of Paterson, N. J., and sold by him to JOHN A. TAINTOR; sold by Mr. TAINTOR to DANIEL BUCK; sold by D. BUCK to S. W. ROBBINS, Wethersfield, Conn., and by him butchered.

WM. BUCK. **20 Snowberry,**

Sire ————————; Dam SNOWFLAKE (16).

WM. BUCK.—S. R. G. **21 Waterbury,**

Sire WIDE AWAKE (19); Dam CLOVER 2d, (17); birth April 5th, 1862; bred by DANIEL BUCK; sold by F. L. WRIGHT to

E. L. DUNBAR; owned by WM. BROWN in 1863; slaughtered by E. L. DUNBAR in Fall of 1865.

S. R. G. **22 Reindeer,**

Sire WATERBURY 21; Dam SNOWFLAKE 9; birth February 28th, 1866; bred by S. R. GRIDLEY; sold by him to WM. BULL, Plymouth, Conn.

S. W. R.—J. T. N. **23 Brice,**

Imported by WM. REDMOND, of N. Y.

J. T. N. **24 Comet,**

Sire BRICE 23; Dam ANGELINA BAKER 21.

J. T. N. **25 McClellan,**

Sire COMET 24; Dam ANGELINA BAKER 21; black and white; bred by WM. REDMOND, of N. Y.

J. T. N.—S. W. R.—W. B. **26 Living Storm,**

Sire MCCLELLAN 25; Dam PANSY 22; birth March 20th, 1864; black, brown and white; bred by JOHN T. NORTON; bought by WALLACE BARNES of S. W. ROBBINS, in March, 1864, and now owned by W. BARNES, Bristol, Conn.

S. R. G. **27 Fortune,**

Sire ——— (10); Dam VIOLET (25); bred by ELISHA COLT, and sold by him to S. R. GRIDLEY; butchered by GAD LEWIS, Bristol, Conn.

S. R. G. **28 Bill,**

Sire FORTUNE 27; Dam CLOVER 27; birth July 4th, 1860; bred by S. R. GRIDLEY; sold by him July, 1860, to JOHN L. MERRILS, New Hartford.

E. L. D. **29 Non Est,**

Sire EMPEROR 2d, 7; Dam CLOVER 27; birth May, 1861; bred by E. L. DUNBAR; slaughtered a calf.

E. L. D. **30 General Grant,**

Sire PRINCE 8; Dam CLOVER 27; birth November 1862; bred by E. L DUNBAR; sold by him in April 1864, to O. I. MARTIN, Wallingford, Conn.

E. L. D. **31 Gone,**

Sire RAGHORN 5; Dam CLOVER 27; birth 1863; bred by E. L. DUNBAR; slaughtered when a calf, by him.

F. L. W. **32 April Fool,**

Sire RAGHORN 5; Dam CLOVER 2d 17; birth April 1st, 1863; bred by Dr. F. L. WRIGHT, Bristol, Conn.; slaughtered a calf, by SYLVESTER HART.

W. B. **33 Connecticut,**

Sire LIVING STORM 26; Dam ANGELINE 31; birth March 26th, 1866; bred by W. BARNES; sold AVERY ATKINS, May 18th, 1866.

(JERSEY HERD RECORD.) **34 Halicarnassus,**

Calved 1862; bred by DAVID LEAVITT, JR., Great Barrington, Mass., from JOHN A. TAINTOR stock; bought by E. L. DUNBAR in Spring of 1867, of Mr. HANMAR, of East Hartford. (36 Brook's Jersey Herd Record.)

W. B. **35 Blade,**

Sire RAGHORN 5; Dam SUKEY 36; birth Feb. 1st, 1863; bred by W. BARNES; sold A. J. WHITTEMORE, and slaughtered a calf.

H. B. D. **36 Tom Thumb,**

Sire LIVING STORM 26; Dam SUKEY 36; birth March 15th, 1866; bred by H. B. DODGE; sold by him to JOSEPH M. WATERS, November 19th, 1866.

3

H. B. D. **37 Diaz,**

Sire LIVING STORM 26; Dam SUKEY 36; birth March 25th, 1867; bred by H. B. DODGE; sold by W. BARNES, October 12, 1867, to GEO. I. HADSELL.

H. B. D. **38 Reverse,**

Sire LIVING STORM 26; Dam SUKEY 36; birth May 11th, 1868; bred by H. B. DODGE; died a calf.

S. R. G. **39 Jack,**

Sire RAGHORN 5; Dam FAWN 37; birth January 20th, 1661; bred by S. R. GRIDLEY; slaughtered when a calf.

M. W. **40 Repent,**

Sire LIVING STORM 26; Dam FAWN 37; birth 1866; bred by MERRITT WARNER; died a calf.

W. BULL. **41 Mingo,**

Sire REINDEER 22; Dam FAWN 37; birth March 20th, 1868; bred by WM. BULL; sold June 3d, 1868, to J. L. MERRILL, New Hartford, for native cows.

J. H. S. **42 Prince 2d,**

Sire PRINCE 8; Dam DAISY 13; birth August 6th, 1864; bred by J. H. SUTLIFF; owned by Dr. WM. H. SMITH.

E. A. N. **43 Phil Sheridan,**

Sire LIVING STORM 26; Dam BELLE 45; birth May 6th, 1867; bred by EDGAR A. NORTON.

E. L. D. **44 Role,**

Sire R. M. ANDREWS' Grade Bull; Dam KITTY 38; birth 1862; deaconed; breeding stolen by Bull in Fall of 1861.

E. L. D. **45 Accidental,**

Sire ANDREWS' Grade Ayrshire Bull; Dam KITTY 38; birth 1864; deaconed; breeding stole by Bull.

E. L. D.   **46 Experiment,**

Sire L. H. HOLLISTER's Grade Short Horn; Dam KITTY 38; birth 1865; bred by E. L. DUNBAR; killed a calf.

E. L. D.   **47 Kidd,**

Sire WATERBURY 21; Dam KITTY 38; birth 1866; bred by E. L. DUNBAR.

E. L. D.   **48 Halo,**

Sire HALICARNASSUS 34; Dam KITTY 38; birth 1868; bred by E. L. DUNBAR; killed a calf.

W. H. S.   **49 Joe Hooker,**

Sire PRINCE 8; Dam ROSALIE 55; birth May 7th, 1865; bred by Dr. WM. H. SMITH.

W. H. S.   **50 Victor,**

Sire PRINCE 2d 42; Dam ROSALIE 55; birth May 10th, 1868; bred by Dr. WM. H. SMITH.

E. L. D.   **51 Stafford,**

Sire JOHN A. TAINTOR's Bull; Dam BERGAMOT 61; birth Fall 1859; bred by JOHN A. TAINTOR; sold by E. L. DUNBAR to ANSON L. ATWOOD, Bristol, in 1859.

T. B.—W. B.   **52 Spot,**

Sire EMPEROR 2d 7; Dam BERGAMOT 61; birth March 13th, 1861; bred by THOS. BARNES; castrated in Wolcott.

W. B.   **53 Shambles,**

Sire RAGHORN 5; Dam BERGAMOT 61; birth March, 1863; bred by W. BARNES; slaughtered when a calf.

A. A.—W. B.   **54 Romeo,**

Sire LIVING STORM 26; Dam NELLIE 2d 64; birth April 1866; bred by AVERY ATKINS; now owned by ROBERT CAIRNS, Bristol.

E. L. D.
55 Frank,

Sire RAGHORN 5; Dam LITTLE FAWN 68; birth 1863; bred by E. L. DUNBAR; deaconed.

E. L. D.
56 John,

Sire PRINCE 8; Dam LITTLE FAWN 68; birth 1864; bred by E. L. DUNBAR; deaconed.

E. L. D.
57 Alloy,

Sire L. H. HOLLISTER's Grade Bull; Dam LITTLE FAWN 68; birth 1865; bred by E. L. DUNBAR, deaconed.

E. L. D.
58 Merrit,

Sire HALICARNASSUS 34; Dam LITTLE FAWN 68; birth March 1868; bred by E. L. DUNBAR; deaconed.

R. J.
59 Mars,

Sire LIVING STORM 26; Dam FANNY FAWN 70; birth Aug. 17th, 1868; bred by RUSSELL JUDSON.

W. B.
60 Duke,

Sire RAGHORN 5; Dam FANNY 67; birth February 11th, 1863; bred by W. BARNES; owned by MUNSON WILCOX.

W. B.
61 Jonathan,

Sire PRINCE 8; Dam FANNY 67; birth January 18th, 1864; bred by W. BARNES; by him sold A. N. MERRICK, Springfield, February 11th, 1864.

W. B.
62 Pete,

Sire RAGHORN 5: Dam DEWDROP 75; birth Feb. 1863; bred by W. BARNES; slaughtered when a calf.

A. J. W.
63 Whit,

Sire GRADE DURHAM; Dam DEWDROP 75; birth Jan. 26, '64; breeding stolen by cow while owned by Dr. A. J. WHITTEMORE deaconed by Mr. Sutliff.

A. R. **64 Sam,**

Sire WATERBURY 21; Dam DEWDROP 75; birth Dec. 5, 1865; bred by ADDISON RUSS; sold to LEWIS & PETTIS, New Britain, Ct.

W. B. **65 Newtown,**

Birth Dec. 25th, 1859; bred by JOHN A. TAINTOR; Dam LILLIE 81; sold by W. BARNES to E. L. DUNBAR, by him to GEO. NORTHROP, Newtown, Ct.

W. B. **66 Bristol,**

Sire EMPEROR 2nd, 7; Dam LILLIE 81; birth Jan., 1861; bred by W. BARNES; sent by E. L. DUNBAR to Ackron, Ohio.

W. B. **67 Young Roger,**

Sire COMMODORE NUTT 15; Dam GRACE 82; birth Sept 12th, 1865; bred by W. BARNES; sold GEO. C. HITCHCOCK, May 2d, 1866, by him to FRANK HALE, Litchfield, Conn.

W. B. **68 Gray Eagle,**

Sire LIVING STORM 26; Dam MINNIE 83; birth Feb. 26th, 1866; bred by W. BARNES; sold Nov. 22d, 1866, to JOHN T. ROCKWELL, Winsted, Ct.

T. B. **69 Simmer,**

Sire EMPEROR 2d; (7); Dam LADY ALDERNEY 84; birth April, 1861; bred by THOS. BARNES; sold AMZI BALL; slaughtered a calf.

J. T. R. **70 Tanner,**

Sire JERSEY 108; Dam LADY ALDERNEY 84; birth April 4, 1866; bred by J. T. ROCKWELL.

J. T. R. **71 Stillman,**

Sire McCLELLAN 25; Dam LADY ALDERNEY 84; birth May 26, 1867; bred by JOHN T. ROCKWELL.

J. T. R. ## 72 Gray Eagle 2d,

Sire GRAY EAGLE 68; Dam LADY ALDERNEY 84; birth March 20, 1868; bred by JOHN T. ROCKWELL; owned by FRANK J. KILBOURNE, Litchfield, Ct.

J. T. R. ## 73 Hemlock,

Sire JERSEY 108; Dam DAISEY 87; birth April 3, 1866; bred by JOHN T. ROCKWELL.

J. T. R. ## 74 White Oak,

Sire GRAY EAGLE 68; Dam DAISEY 87; birth Mar. 11, 1868; bred by JOHN T. ROCKWELL.

J. T. R. ## 75 Jupiter,

GRAY, FAWN AND WHITE,

Sire GRAY EAGLE 68; Dam CLOVER 89; birth July 5, 1868; bred by JOHN T. ROCKWELL.

J. H. S. ## 76 Commodore,

Sire RAGHORN 5; Dam ROSALIE 55; birth June 26, 1863; bred by J. H. SUTLIFF; sold by him, in June, 1863, to RUSSELL JUDSON.

J. H. S.—W. H. S. ## 77 Star,

Sire RAGHORN 5; Dam DAISEY 13; birth Sept. 4, 1863; bred by JOHN H. SUTLIFF; sold to Dr. WM. H. SMITH.

T. B. ## 78 Lost,

Sire RAGHORN 5; Dam MIGNIONETTE 11; birth March, 1860; bred by THOMAS BARNES; Presented to J. H. SUTLIFF; died a calf.

WM. A. GUILD. ## 79 Major,

Imported by Mr. CUSHING of Belmont.

W. A. G.   **80 Colonel,**

Sire MAJOR 79; Dam ———; imported by Mr. CUSHING; owned by E. M. READ, Tewksbury, Mass.

W. A. G.   **81 Duke,**

Sire DICK SWIVELLER 112; Dam THOS. MOTLEY'S Cow.

W. A. G.   **82 Jerry,**

Sire COLONEL 80; Dam PHŒBE 91; bred by WM. A. GUILD, Bedford, Mass.

W. A. G.   **83 Pequabock,**

Sire JERRY 82; Dam DAHLIA 93; birth March 17, 1868; bred by WM. A. GUILD; now owned by S. N. HART, Southington, Ct.

WM. GODDARD.   **84 Challenger,**

Sire thorough bred Bull "LORD LONSDALE;" owned by LONSDALE Co., Providence, R. I.; Dam JESSIE 131.

W. G.   **85 Competitor,**

Imported by WM. GODDARD, Providence, R. I.

W. G.   **86 Narragansett,**

Sire CHALLENGER 84; Dam FLORA 2d, 94; birth Oct. 1867; bred by WM. GODDARD, Providence, R. I.

J. H. S.   **87 Adventure,**

Sire BRADLEY & WEBSTER's Bull; Dam DOLLY 96; birth April 13, 1859; bred by J. H. SUTLIFF; sold to LUTHER TUTTLE.

J. H. S.   **88 Brickbat,**

Sire EMPEROR 2d 7; Dam DOLLY 96; birth Feb. 23, 1860; bred by J. H. SUTLIFF; killed a Calf by HENRY PECK.

J. H. S.   **89 Cæsar,**

Sire RAGHORN 7; Dam DOLLY 96; birth Dec. 26, 1860; bred by J. H. SUTLIFF; died a Calf.

J. H. S.   **90 Sam,**

Sire COMMODORE NUTT 15; Dam DOLLY 2d 97; birth March 5, 1864; bred by J. H. SUTLIFF; killed a Calf by HENRY PECK.

J. H. S.   **91 Julien,**

Sire ROMEO 54; Dam DOLLY 2d 97; birth Oct. 23, 1868; bred by J. H. SUTLIFF; owned by B. S. BEACH, Terryville, Ct.

J. H. S.—R. D. H. A.   **92 Ulysses,**

Sire ROMEO 54; Dam DAISY 99; birth Nov. 20, 1868; bred by J. H. SUTLIFF; owned by R. D. H. ALLEN, Terryville, Ct.

S. R. G.   **93 Harwinton,**

Sire DAN BUCK, JR., 11; Dam VIOLET 103; birth April 2, 1862; bred by S. R. GRIDLEY; sold to J. R. BRADLEY, Harwinton, Ct.

S. R. G.   **94 Baltimore,**

Sire JACK 16; Dam VIOLET 103; birth May 21, 1864; bred by S. R. GRIDLEY; slaughtered a Calf.

F. R.   **95 Splendid Jr.,**

Sire SPLENDID 4; Dam LADY STANLEY 106; owned by FRANKLIN RHODES, New Britain, Ct.

WM. BRADLEY.   **96 Dan,**

YELLOW.

Sire SPLENDID, JR. 95; Dam HENRY RUSSELL'S PEGGY; bred by JOHN GILES; birth 1866.

E. C.   **97 Tommy,**

Sire DAN 96; Dam ———; birth March, 1867; bred by EGBERT COWLES; sold by Mr. COWLES to E. L. DUNBAR in Spring of 1868; now owned by GEO. GRIDLEY.

P. W. H.   **98 Clifton,**

Imported in 1865 by R. W. CAMERON of New York; now owned by P. W. HUDSON, North Manchester, Ct.

W. B.—P. W. H.   **99 Oakland,**

Sire COMMODORE NUTT 15; Dam COWSLIP 28; bred by W. BARNES; owned by P. W. HUDSON.

P. W. H.   **100 Dick,**

Sire OAKLAND 99; Dam BUTTER CUP 2d 110; bred by P. W. HUDSON, North Manchester, Ct.

EDWIN MERRIT.   **101 Bill,**

Imported by Col. SAMUEL COLT in Aug., 1859; slaughtered in winter of 1861 and 1862.

P. W. HUDSON.   **102 Bashan,**

Sire BILL 101; Dam VIOLET 25; bred by ELISHA COLT, Hartford, Ct.

P. W. H.   **103 Uncas,**

Sire OAKLAND 99; Dam CLOVER 120; bred by P. W. HUD-SON; owned by W. H. YEOMANS.

W. G.   **104 Climax,**

Sire thoroughbred Bull LORD LONSDALE; owned by LONSDALE Co.; Dam FLORA 94; birth 1866; bred by WM. GODDARD: owned by H. W. BASSET, Derby, Ct.

4

E. C.   **105 Eureka,**

Sire CLIMAX 104; Dam BESS 122; birth Jan. 25, 1869; bred by EGBERT COWLES; color fawn, with two white spots on the belly.

CLINTON W. COWLES.   **106 Prince,**

Sire from JOHN A. TAINTOR'S stock; Dam a daughter of JENNY 2d, by McCLELLAN 25.

E. A. N.   **107 Burdell,**

Sire LIVING STORM 26; Dam BELLE 45; birth Feb. 7, 1869; bred by EDGAR A. NORTON.

J. T. R.   **108 Jersey,**

Sire BILL 28; Dam BUTTER CUP 134; birth Sept. 5, 1862; bred by H. E. DAY, Hartford, Ct., and sold to H. B. DEWOLF; sold to WM. E. COWLES, Winsted, Ct.; sold to GEORGE ADAMS, M. D., North Canaan, Ct., Nov. 14, 1865; by him slaughtered Jan. 3, 1867.

J. T. R.   **109 Prize,**

Sire GRAY EAGLE 68; Dam LADY ALDERNEY 84; birth March 6, 1869; bred by JOHN T. ROCKWELL.

J. H. S.   **110 Charles,**

Sire TAINTOR's Bull; Dam SUE 26; birth 1859; bred by J. A. TAINTOR; presented by E. L. DUNBAR to J. H. SUTLIFF; sold at seven months old to V. ATKINS for native use.

J. T. R.   **111 Xiphias,**

Sire GRAY EAGLE 68; Dam DAISY 87; birth March 13, 1869; bred by JOHN T. ROCKWELL; sold by N. T. BALDWIN to W. BARNES.

G. FROST.   **112 Dick Swiveller,**

Sire MAJOR 113; Dam T. MOTLEY's imported FLORA; owned by THOS. MOTLEY.

G. F. **113 Major,**

Sire COLONEL 114; Dam T. MOTLEY's imported COUNTESS; owned by THOS. MOTLEY.

G. F. **114 Colonel,**

Imported by THOMAS MOTLEY in 1851; first premium Bull from Col. LE COUTER's Cow BEAUTY.

A. BARTHOLOMEW. **115 Napoleon,**

Sire MAJOR 113; Dam BRENDA 135.

E. M. REED. **116 Comet,**

Sire NAPOLEON 115; Dam DUCHESS 136; birth April 23, 1856; owned by E. M. REED.

W. BARNES. **117 Yok,**

Sire LIVING STORM 26; Dam DAHLIA 93; birth March 22, 1869; bred by W. BARNES.

W. B. DINSMORE. **118 Bismarck,**

Color gray, fawn, and some white; black switch; birth June, 1867; bred on Island of Jersey; imported by W. B. DINSMORE, on ship New World, and landed at New York Nov. 16, 1868; now owned by WALLACE BARNES, Bristol, Ct.

T. & B.—D. B. **119 Splendens,**

Imported by TAINTOR & BUCK, 1851; owned by DAN'L BUCK.

The following corrections were received too late to be made in their proper place:

S. R. G. **10 Jack Frost,**

Sire SPLENDENS 119; Dam JESSIE 146.

S. R. G. **27 Fortune,**

Sire JACK FROST 10.

COWS.

J. T. NORTON. **1 Daisy,**

Imported from Isle of Jersey, by JOHN A. TAINTOR, in August, 1852, age sixteen months; bought, on arrival at Hartford, Conn., by JOHN T. NORTON; sold to WALTER M. HUNGERFORD, Wolcottville, Conn., Sept. 25, 1855.

J. T. N. **2 Jenny,**

Imported from Isle of Jersey, by JOHN A. TAINTOR, of Hartford, Conn., via Havre, in August, 1852; bought, on arrival at Hartford, by JOHN T. NORTON.

W. M. H. **3 Rose,**

Sire SPLENDID (4); Dam DAISY (1); birth April 14, 1857; bred by W. M. HUNGERFORD, and sold by him to S. R. GRIDLEY, Bristol, Conn., Dec. 20, 1858; sold by S. R. GRIDLEY to WALLACE BARNES, Bristol, Conn., May 21, 1868.

T. M. STOUGHTON. **4 Winonia,**

Imported from Isle of Jersey, by JONATHAN BIRD, of Bellville, N. J.

T. M. S. **5 Fawn, otherwise Neocomis,**

Imported in the Cow WINONIA (4.)

S. R. G.

6 Flirt,

Sire EMPEROR 2d (7); Dam ROSE (3); birth March 20, 1860; bred by S. R. GRIDLEY; sold to E. L. DUNBAR, June 22, 1861, and by him to W. BARNES, and by him, Feb'y 15, 1864, to JAMES O. SHELDON, Geneva, N. Y.; served by PRINCE (8,) Sept. 2, 1863.

J. H. S.

7 Blanche,

Imported in Dam, by JOHN A. TAINTOR; bought by JOHN H. SUTLIFF, Bristol, Conn., May 4, 1859; sold by him to MARTIN GOLDSBOROUGH, Baltimore, Md.

S. W. R.

8 Clover,

Imported for DAN'L BUCK, by J. A. TAINTOR; slaughtered by S. W. ROBBINS, Wethersfield, Conn.

S. R. G.

9 Snow Flakes,

Sire DAN BUCK, Jr., (11); Dam ROSE (3); birth April 5, 1862; bred by S. R. GRIDLEY.

S. R. G.

10 Tabby,

Sire RAGHORN (5); Dam ROSE (3); birth March 31, 1863; bred by S. R. GRIDLEY, and sold to DAN'L BUCK in 1864.

T. B.

11 Mignionette,

Imported in Dam MARY, by J. A. TAINTOR; bought May 4, 1859, by THOS. BARNES.

S. R. G.

12 Baptist,

Sire COMMODORE NUTT (15); Dam ROSE (3); birth June 9, 1866, in a brook, and drowned; bred by S. R. GRIDLEY.

J. H. S.   ## 13 Daisy,

Sire EMPEROR 2d (7); Dam BLANCHE (7); birth Nov. 28, 1860; bred by JOHN H. SUTLIFF; sold to Dr. WM. H. SMITH, in 1863.

E. L. D.   ## 14 Kitty,

Sire DAN BUCK, Jr., (11); Dam FLIRT (6); birth Feb., 1862; bred by E. L. DUNBAR; sold by J. H. AUSTIN to JOHN T. GOMME, Sept 21, 1866; in Calf by LIVING STORM (26.)

E. L. D.   ## 15 Cherry,

Sire RAGHORN (5); Dam FLIRT (6); birth 1863; bred by E. L. DUNBAR; sold by W. BARNES to JAS. O. SHELDON, Feb. 15, 1864.

WM. BUCK.   ## 16 Snow Flakes,

Sire FOUR O'CLOCK IN THE MORNING, *alias* BOSTONY; bred by HENSHAW, of Philadelphia, Penn.; Dam WHITE HEART, out of a Cow imported by J. A. TAINTOR, in 1851.

WM. BUCK.   ## 17 Clover 2d,

Sire SNOWBERRY 20; Dam CLOVER (8); birth 1859; bred by DANIEL BUCK; sold by him to S. R. GRIDLEY; sold by W. BARNES, May 8, 1868, to WM. BULL.

S. R. G.   ## 18 Plade,

Sire JACK 16; Dam SNOW FLAKES (9); birth May 1, 1864; bred by S. R. GRIDLEY; died a Calf.

S. R. G.   ## 19 Dolly,

Sire COMMODORE NUTT 15; Dam SNOW FLAKES 9; birth April 10, 1865; bred by S. R. GRIDLEY; sold to GEORGE C. HITCHCOCK, New Preston, Conn.; now in Calf by THORNE.

S. R. G.
20 Daisy,
Twin to DOLLY 19; owned by GEO. C. HITCHCOCK.

J. T. N.
21 Angelina Baker,
Imported by ROSWELL L. COLT, of Paterson, N. J.

J. T. N.
22 Pansy,
Imported by JOHN A. TAINTOR, for JOHN T. NORTON, from the Island of Jersey, via Havre, by Ship Southampton, October 11, 1855.

S. R. G.
23 June,
Sire LIVING STORM 26; Dam SNOW FLAKES 9; birth June 19, 1867; bred by S. R. GRIDLEY; color fawn and white.

S. R. G.
24 Crocus,
Sire LIVING STORM 26; Dam SNOW FLAKES 9; birth April 8, 1868; bred by S. R. GRIDLEY; now owned by MUNSON WILCOX, Bristol, Conn.

E. C.
25 Violet,
Imported by JOHN A. TAINTOR; sold by AUSTIN DUNHAM to ELISHA COLT in 1853.

J. A. T.
26 Sue,
Imported in Dam ———, by JOHN A. TAINTOR; bought, at six years old, of JOHN A. TAINTOR, by ALBERT A. BRADLEY, July 14, 1858; sold by BRADLEY, in 1858, to E. L. DUNBAR: sold by him to S. S. SHERWOOD, Paterson, N. J.

J. A. T.—S. R. G.
27 Clover,
Imported from Isle of Jersey, by JOHN A. TAINTOR, in 1855; birth on shipboard; sold to S. R. GRIDLEY in 1858; sold by S.

R. Gridley to E. L. Dunbar; now owned by Egbert Cowles, Farmington, Conn.

s. r. g. **28 Cowslip,**

Sire Fortune 27; Dam Clover 27; birth June 16, 1859; bred by S. R. Gridley; sold to W. Barnes, March 17, 1860; sold by him, June 3, 1863, to Daniel Buck; sold by him to P. W. Hudson; by him sold to J. B. Williams, Glastenbury, Conn.

e. l. d. **29 Grade,**

Sire L. H. Hollister's grade, short horn Bull; Dam Clover 27; birth March, 1865; bred by E. L. Dunbar, and sold to William Lewis, May 29, 1865.

w. b. **30 Flora,**

Sire Dan Buck, Jr., 11; Dam Cowslip 28; birth March 24, 1862, (her first calf;) bred by W. Barnes; sold, Oct 20, 1863, to Edw'd O. Eaton, Troy, N. Y.; in Calf by Prince 8.

f. l. w. **31 Angeline,**

Sire Prince 8; Dam Clover, 2d, 17; birth Feb. 26, 1864; bred by Doct. F. L. Wright; sold by W. Barnes to John T. Gomme, Lexington, Ky., Sept. 21, 1866.

f. l. w. **32 Camelia,**

Sire Commodore Nutt 15; Dam Clover, 2d, 17; birth March 5th, 1865; bred by Doct. F. L. Wright; sold by W. Barnes, Aug. 28, 1865, to Jas. O. Sheldon.

f. l. w. **33 Cactus,**

Sire Living Storm 26; Dam Clover, 2d, 17; birth March 1, 1866; bred by Dr. F. L Wright; sold by W. Barnes, Sept. 21, 1866, to John T. Gomme.

F. L. W.   **34 Daisy,**

Sire LIVING STORM 26; Dam CLOVER, 2d, 17; birth Jan'y 22, 1867; bred by Dr. F. L. WRIGHT; owned by ADISON RUSS.

W. B.   **35 Disappointment,**

Sire LIVING STORM 26; Dam CLOVER, 2d, 17; birth Jan. 10, 1868; bred by W. BARNES; died a calf.

J. A. T.—S. R. G.   **36 Sukey,**

Imported from Isle of Jersey, by JOHN A. TAINTOR, and sold to S. R. GRIDLEY of Bristol, Conn., in summer of 1858, at six years old; died in 1868,—having produced six Heifer and four Bull Calves: the last one being REVERSE (38.)

S. R. G.   **37 Fawn,**

Sire SPLENDID 4; Dam SUKEY 3; birth March 2d, 1859; bred by JOHN A. TAINTOR; now owned by WM. BULL, Plymouth, Conn.

S. R. G.   **38 Kitty,**

Sire EMPEROR, 2d, 7; Dam SUKEY 36; birth March 13th, 1860; bred by S. R. GRIDLEY.

S. R. G.   **39 Delight,**

Sire RAGHORN 5; Dam SUKEY 36; birth March 5, 1861; bred by S. R. GRIDLEY; sold by him to DANIEL BUCK, May 16th, 1864.

W. B.   **40 Susie,**

Sire DAN BUCK, Jr., 11; Dam SUKEY 36; birth Jan'y 31st, 1862; bred by W. BARNES; sold, Feb. 11, 1864, to A. N. MERRICK, Springfield, Mass.; in Calf by JACK (16.)

H. B. D. ## 41 Flirt,

Sire COMMODORE NUTT 15; Dam SUKEY 36; birth Jan. 27th, 1864; bred by H. B. DODGE; sold by him, Nov. 19th, 1866, to JOSEPH M. WATERS; now owned by J. B. POWELL, West Hartford, Conn.

H. B. D. ## 42 Juno,

Sire COMMODORE NUTT 15; Dam SUKEY 36; birth March, 1865; bred by H. B. DODGE; died in May, 1865.

S. R. G. ## 43 Surprise, .

Sire DAN BUCK, Jr., 11; Dam FAWN 37; birth Nov. 29th, 1861; bred by S. R. GRIDLEY; sold to A. J. WHITTEMORE, and died without issue.

E. L. D.—W. B. ## 44 Magnolia,

Sire COMMODORE NUTT 15; Dam FAWN 37; birth April 9th, 1863; bred by E. L. DUNBAR; sold by W. BARNES to Dr. WM. H. SMITH, Newport, R. I.

M. W. ## 45 Belle,

Sire COMMODORE NUTT 15; Dam FAWN 37; birth June 16th, 1864; bred by MERRITT WARNER, Terryville, Ct.; now owned by EDGAR A. NORTON, Bristol, Ct.

M. W. ## 46 Miss Take,

Sire DEVON BULL; Dam FAWN 37; birth 1865; bred by MERRITT WARNER.

E. A. N.—W. B. ## 47 Snowdrop,

Sire LIVING STORM 26; Dam FAWN 37; birth March 10th, 1867; bred by EDGAR A. NORTON; sold to GEORGE C. HITCHCOCK, April 23, 1867.

W. H. S.   # 48 Topsey,

Sire JACK 16; Dam MAGNOLIA 44; birth April 12, 1865; bred by Dr. WM. H. SMITH.

W. H. S.   # 49 Lizzie,

Sire PRINCE, 2d, 42; Dam MAGNOLIA 44; birth January 28, 1868; bred by Dr. WM. H. SMITH.

M. W.   # 50 Belle Isle,

Sire LIVING STORM 26; Dam BELLE 45; birth May 15th, 1866; bred by MERRITT WARNER; sold by W. BARNES to JOHN T. GOMME.

E. A. N.—W. B.   # 51 Chamois,

Sire LIVING STORM 26; Dam BELLE 45; birth March 20th, 1868; bred by EDGAR A. NORTON; sold May 8th, 1868, by W. BARNES, to WM. BULL.

E. L. D.   # 52 Jane,

Sire RAGHORN 5; Dam KITTY 38; birth 1863; bred by E. L. DUNBAR, Bristol, Conn.; sold by RUSSEL JUDSON to Dr. J. M. RIGGS, Hartford, Conn.

E. L. D.   # 53 Hellen,

Sire LIVING STORM 26; Dam KITTY 38; birth March, 1867; bred and owned by E. L. DUNBAR.

H. B. D.   # 54 Fern,

Sire LIVING STORM 26; Dam FLIRT 41; birth Feb. 15th, 1866; bred by H. B. DODGE; sold to JOHN T. GOMME, Sept. 21st, 1866, by W. BARNES.

J. H. S.—W. H. S.   ## 55 Rosalie,

Sire EMPEROR, 2d, 7; Dam BLANCHE 7; birth Oct. 16, 1861; bred by JOHN H. SUTLIFF; sold to Dr. WM. H. SMITH, Newport, R. I.

W. H. S.   ## 56 Janet,

Sire PRINCE 8; Dam ROSALIE 55; birth March 27, 1866; bred by Dr. WM. H. SMITH, R. I.

W. H. S.   ## 57 Blossom,

Sire PRINCE, 2d, 42; Dam ROSALIE 55; birth March 5, 1867; bred by Dr. WM. H. SMITH.

W. H. S.   ## 58 Nellie,

Sire PRINCE, 2d, 42; Dam TOPSEY 48; birth June 14, 1867; bred by Dr. WM. H. SMITH.

W. H. S.   ## 59 Inez,

Sire PRINCE 8; Dam DAISY 13; birth July 4th, 1866; bred by Dr. WM. H. SMITH.

W. H. S.   ## 60 Effie,

Sire JOE HOOKER 49; Dam DAISY 13; birth Feb. 20, 1868; bred by Dr. WM. H. SMITH.

M. GOLDSBOROUGH.   ## 61 Bergamot,

Imported in Dam by JOHN A. TAINTOR; bought, May 4th, 1859, by DUNBAR & BARNES, for E. L. DUNBAR; sold by W. BARNES, to JAS. O. SHELDON, Feb. 15, 1864.

W. B.   ## 62 Nellie,

Sire EMPEROR, 2d, 7; Dam BERGAMOT 61; birth Jan. 23d, 1862; bred by W. BARNES; sold to JOHN GILES, June 6, 1865.

W. B.   ## 63 Irene,

Sire COMMODORE NUTT 15; Dam BERGAMOT 61; birth Jan'y 2d, 1864; bred by W. BARNES; sold by him to JAS. O. SHELDON, Feb. 15th, 1864.

E. L. D.   ## 64 Nellie 2d,

Sire PRINCE 8; Dam NELLIE 62; birth April 3d, 1864; bred by E. L. DUNBAR; sold by AVERY ATKINS, to go to ——— New York.

W. B.   ## 65 Marigold,

Sire COMMODORE NUTT 15; Dam NELLIE 62; drop'd April 28, 1865; bred by W. BARNES; sold by W. BARNES, Aug. 28, 1865, to JAS. O. SHELDON.

E. L. D.   ## 66 Lady Alice,

Sire EMPEROR, 2d, 7; Dam SUE 26; birth March 7th, 1860; bred by E. L. DUNBAR; sold to JAS. O. SHELDON, Feb'y 15th, 1864; in Calf, by GEN. GRANT 30, Aug. 7th, 1863.

J. A. T.—W. B.   ## 67 Fanny,

Nearly all fawn color; birth April, 1859; bought, March 19, 1860, by WALLACE BARNES, of JOHN A. TAINTOR; purity of blood verified by Mr. TAINTOR, who imported her Sire and Grand Dam.

W. B.   ## 68 Little Fawn,

Sire J. A. TAINTOR's Bull; Dam FANNY 67; birth Dec. 26th, 1860; bred by JOHN A. TAINTOR; owned by E. L. DUNBAR, Bristol, Conn.

E. L. D.   ## 69 Little Fanny,

Sire RAGHORN 5; Dam LITTLE FAWN 68; birth Aug. 10th, 1862; bred by E. L. DUNBAR, by him sold to Dr. WM. H. SMITH.

E. L. D.   **70 Fanny Fawn,**

Sire WATERBURY 21; Dam LITTLE FAWN 68; birth 1866; bred by E. L. DUNBAR, and by him sold to RUSSEL JUDSON, Bristol, Conn.

E. L. D.   **71 Fawnette,**

Sire LIVING STORM 26; Dam LITTLE FAWN 68; birth 1867; bred by E. L. DUNBAR; by him sold to R. D. H. ALLEN, Terryville, Ct.

W. H. S.   **72 Pansy,**

Sire PRINCE, 2d, 42; Dam LITTLE FANNY 69; birth Jan'y 24th, 1867; bred by Dr. WM. H. SMITH.

W. B.   **73 Lily,**

Sire EMPEROR, 2d, 7; Dam FANNY 67; birth Feb. 9th, 1862; bred by W. BARNES; by him sold, Oct. 20th, 1863, to EDW'D O. EATON, Troy, N. Y.; in Calf by COM. NUTT 15; now owned by J. MILTON MACKIE, Gt. Barrington, Mass.

J. A. T.—W. B.   **74 Fate,**

Birth April, 1859; light fawn, and white,—broken horn; bought of JOHN A. TAINTOR by WALLACE BARNES, March 19, 1860; died in pasture without issue.

J. A. T.—W. B.   **75 Dew Drop,**

Two Teats only; birth July, 1859; bought, March 19, 1860, by WALLACE BARNES of JOHN A. TAINTOR; purity of blood verified by him.

W. B.   **76 Meekness,**

Sire EMPEROR, 2d, 7; Dam DEW DROP 75; birth Jan. 26th, 1862; bred by W. BARNES,

J. H. S.   **77 Lantana,**

Sire GEN. GRANT 30; Dam DEW DROP 75; birth Dec. 1st, 1864; bred by JOHN H. SUTLIFF; sold by A. RUSS to J. O. SHELDON, Aug. 28, 1865.

A. R.   **78 Rose,**

Sire WATERBURY 21; Dam DEW DROP 75; birth Nov. 1st, 1866; bred by A. RUSS; last live Calf of DEW DROP to January, 1869.

W. B.   **79 Mattie,**

Sire COMMODORE NUTT 15; Dam MEEKNESS 76; birth Feb. 20th, 1864; bred by W. BARNES.

A. R.   **80 Lucelle,**

Sire ROMEO 54; Dam ROSE 78; birth Dec. 24, 1868; bred by A. RUSS; (died.)

M. G.—W. B.   **81 Lillie,**

Birth Feb. 10th, 1858; imported in Dam by J. A. TAINTOR; bought, May 4th, 1859, by DUNBAR & BARNES, for WALLACE BARNES; sold, ——, 1862, to O. B. NORTH; in Calf by RAGHORN 5.

W. B.   **82 Grace,**

Sire EMPEROR, 2d, 7; Dam LILLIE 81; birth Jan. 24, 1862; bred by WALLACE BARNES; sold, June 12th, 1866, to MARTIN GOLDSBOROUGH, Baltimore, Md.

W. B.   **83 Minnie,**

Sire COMMODORE NUTT 15; Dam GRACE 82; birth Feb. 19, 1864; bred by W. BARNES; sold to MARTIN GOLDSBOROUGH, Baltimore, Md., June 12, 1866.

T. B.   **84 Lady Alderney,**

Birth 1859; bought by THOS. BARNES, March 19th, 1860, of JOHN A. TAINTOR; purity of blood verified by him; sold by

W. Barnes, Aug. 22, 1863, to John T. Rockwell, Winsted, Conn., and now owned by him.

T. B.—W. B. **85 Blanche,**

Sire Emperor, 2d, 7; Dam Lady Alderney 84; birth Apr., 1862; bred by Thos. Barnes; sold to R. Judson, July 9th, 1862; sold by W. Barnes, Oct. 20, 1863, to Edw'd O. Eaton, Troy, N. Y.; in Calf by Prince 8.

T. B. **86 Emily,**

Sire Raghorn 5; Dam Lady Alderney 84; birth April, 1863; bred by Thos. Barnes; sold to Daniel Buck, June 3d, 1863.

T. B. **87 Daisy,**

Sire Prince 8; Dam Lady Alderney 84; birth March 8th, 1864; bred by Thos. Barnes; sold, Sept. 14th, 1868, by W. Barnes to N. T. Baldwin.

J. T. R. **88 Martha,**

Sire Jersey 108; Dam Lady Alderney 84; birth 1865; bred by John T. Rockwell; owned by Erastus Corning, Albany, N. Y.

J. T. R. **89 Clover,**

FAWN AND WHITE.

Sire McClellan 25; Dam Daisy 87; birth April 19, 1867; bred by John T. Rockwell.

J. T. R. **90 Cream Pot, XIIII.**

Color fawn, yellow and white; bred on the Island of Jersey; imported on ship Gen. McClellan, to New York, Sept. 4, 1868, at two years and four months old, by Thomas Clarendon, of Orange, N. J.; sold by him to John T. Rockwell, Winsted, Conn.; branded, when a yearling, S. O. A. S., by St. Owen's Ag. Society.

W. A. G.   **91 Phœbe,**   (176.—J. H. R.)

Sire DUKE 81; Dam BRENDA; G. Dam BRENDA; imported by MASS. AG. SOCIETY.

T. B.   **92 Dust,**

Sire DAN BUCK, JR., 11; Dam MIGNIONETTE 11; birth Apr. 14, 1862; bred by THOS. BARNES; sold by W. BARNES to E. L. DUNBAR; died a Calf.

W. B.   **93 Dahlia,**

Sire RAGHORN 5; Dam MIGNIONETTE 11; birth April 10th, 1863; bred by W. BARNES; sold to WM. A. GUILD; re-sold, 1867, to W. BARNES.

W. G.   **94 Flora 2d,**

Sire COMPETITOR 85; Dam FLORA 95; bred by WM. GODDARD, Providence, R. I.

W. G.   **95 Flora,**

Imported by WILLIAM GODDARD, Providence, R. I., in June, 1860.

WM. B.—S. R. G.   **96 Dolly,**

BROWN AND DRAB.

Sire SPLENDENS—imported by DANIEL BUCK; Dam DOTT—imported by DANIEL BUCK; bought, 1858, by ALBERT A. BRADLEY of DAVID COLLINS; sold, July, 1858, to JOHN H. SUTLIFF; died March 7, 1862.

J. H. S.   **97 Dolly 2d,**

Sire EMPEROR, 2d, 7; Dam DOLLY 96; birth March 7, 1862; bred by J. H. SUTLIFF; sold, Oct. 10th, 1868, to B. S. BEACH, Terryville, Conn.

J. H. S.   # 98   Nellie,

Sire ——————; Dam DOLLY, 2d, 97 ; birth Jan. 22, 1865 ; bred by J. H. SUTLIFF ; died a Calf.

J. H. S.   # 99   Daisy,

Sire WATERBURY 21 ; Dam DOLLY, 2d, 97 ; birth Jan. 28th, 1866 ; bred by J. H. SUTLIFF ; sold, Oct. 10th, 1868, to R. D. H. ALLEN, Terryville, Conn.

J. H. S.   # 100   Pansy,

Sire LIVING STORM 26 ; Dam DOLLY, 2d, 97 ; birth Dec. 13, 1866 ; bred by J. H. SUTLIFF.

J. H. S.   .   # 101   Rosy,

Sire SAM 64 ; Dam DOLLY, 2d, 97 ; birth Dec. 2, 1867 ; bred by J. H. SUTLIFF.

J. H. S.   # 102   Lilly,

Sire ROMEO 54 ; Dam PANSY 100 ; birth Sept. 22d, 1868 ; bred by J. H. SUTLIFF.

D. B.—S. R. G.   # 103   Violet,

BLACK.

Bred by DANIEL BUCK ; birth ——, 1859 ; Dam D. BUCK's DAISY ; she was out of Imported Stock on both sides ; served, May 12th, 1865, by WATERBURY 21, and sold to A. A. BRADLEY.

S. R. G.   # 104   Polly,

Sire COMMODORE NUTT 15 ; Dam VIOLET 103 ; birth June 30th, 1863 ; bred by S. R. GRIDLEY ; sold to DANIEL BUCK, May 16, 1864.

J. A. T.—S. R. G.　**105 Lillie,**

BROWN HEAD.

Imported by JOHN A. TAINTOR; sold to GEO. LEWIS, Plainville, Conn.

WM. BRADLEY.　**106 Lady Stanley,**

Sire WIDE AWAKE 19; Dam LILLIE, (brown head,) 105.

P. W. HUDSON.　**107 Rose,**

Sire TAINTOR's imported Bull; Dam out of CLOVER 8, by TAINTOR's imported Bull.

P. W. H.　**108 Lilly,**

Sire WIDE AWAKE 19; Dam ROSE 107; bred by DANIEL BUCK, and owned by M. HUDSON.

P. W. H.　**109 Freedom,**

Sire CLIFTON 98; Dam LILLY 108; birth 1868; bred by M. HUDSON; owned by S. D. NEWELL, Bristol, Conn.

P. W. H.—N. L. B.　**110 Butter Cup 2d,**

Sire TAINTOR's Bull; Dam J. A. TAINTOR's imported Cow BUTTER CUP.

P. W. H.—N. L. B.　**111 Butter Cup 3d,**

Sire DICK 100; Dam BUTTER CUP, 2d, 110; birth March 15, 1868; bred by N. L. BIDWELL, So. Coventry, Conn; owned by MUNSON WILCOX.

P. W. H.—N. L. B.　**112 Tanner Cow,**

Bred from Stock sold by JOHN A. TAINTOR to Mr. PAGE, of Norwich, Conn.

P. W. H.—N. L. B. **113 Tanner Heifer,**

Sire BASHAN 102; Dam TANNER Cow 112; bred by WARN-
ER TANNER of Willimantic, Conn.

P. W. H.—N. L. B. **114 Jessamine,**

Sire DICK 100; Dam TANNER HEIFER 112; birth March 22,
1868; bred by N. L. BIDWELL, So. Coventry, Ct.; now owned
by MUNSON WILCOX.

W. H. Y. **115 Nellie 1st,**

Sire ROMP; bred from Stock of TAINTOR's; Dam TANNER
Cow 112.

W. H. Y. **116 Nellie 2d,**

YELLOW.

Sire BASHAN 102; Dam NELLIE, 1st, 115; now owned by
E. L. DUNBAR.

W. H. Y. **117 Nellie 3d,**

YELLOW.

Sire GRAY DICK; bred by C. M. POND, from his Cow CYN-
THA; Dam NELLIE, 2d, 116; bred by WM. H. YEOMANS; owned
by LYMAN A. MILLS, Middlefield, Ct.; in Calf by DAN 96.

W. H. Y. **118 Tulip,**

DARK FAWN AND WHITE.

Sire UNCAS 103; Dam NELLIE, 3d, 117; birth June 20th,
1868: bred by WM. H. YEOMANS; owned by ISAAC P. HART,
Bristol, Conn.

W. H. Y. **119 Hellen Dunbar,**

Sire UNCAS 103; Dam NELLIE, 2d, 116; birth 1868; bred
by WM. H. YEOMANS; owned by LYMAN A. MILLS, Middlefield, Conn.

P. W. H.
120 Clover,

Sire BILL 101; Dam SAM'L COLT's imported Cow; owned by P. W. HUDSON, No. Manchester, Ct.

E. C.
121 Flora,

Bred by H. H. KENT, Valley Falls, R. I.; Dam BETTIE; bred by Hon. DANIEL WEBSTER.

E. COWLES.
122 Bess,

Sire DANIEL; bred by LONSDALE Co., Providence, R. I.; Dam FLORA 121; birth Nov., 1864; bred by LONSDALE Co., Providence, R. I.

F. W. C.
123 Daisy,

Sire BASHAN 102; Dam TULIP 124; birth March, 1863; bred by ELISHA COLT; sold by S. R. GRIDLEY to GEO. GRIDLEY; in Calf by JERSEY; owned by F. W. COWLES, Manchester, Conn.

P. W. H.
124 Tulip,

Sire BILL 101; Dam VIOLET 25; bred by ELISHA COLT; owned by M. HUDSON.

F. W. C.
125 Daisy 2d,

Sire PRINCE 106; Dam DAISY 123; birth Feb. 20th, 1866; bred by F. W. COWLES; owned by MUNSON WILCOX.

E. C.
126 Beauty,

Sire DAN 96; Dam —— from COLT's Stock; bred by EGBERT COWLES; sold to A. RUSS.

E. C.
127 Highhorn,

Sire DAN 96; Dam ——, from ELISHA COLT's Stock; birth Aug., 1867; bred by EGBERT COWLES; owned by CHAS. NORTON, Bristol, Conn.

E. C. **128 Pale Nose,**

Sire DAN 96; Dam ——, from TAINTOR'S Stock; birth Aug.,
1867; bred by EGBERT COWLES; owned by CHAS. NORTON.

J. P. **129 Rose Bud,**

Imported, in 1862, by JAMES PATTEE, Wallingford, Conn.

J. P. **130 Rose Leaf,**

Sire GEN'L GRANT 30; Dam ROSE BUD 129; birth June 21,
1867; bred by JAMES PATTEE.

W. G.—J. C. B. **131 Jessie,**

Imported by WM. GODDARD, Esq., Providence, R. I., in June,
1860; last owned by J. CARTER BROWN, Providence, R. I.

W. BULL. **132 Leah,**

Sire LIVING STORM 26; Dam CLOVER, 2d, 17; birth Feb. 10,
1869; bred by WM. BULL, Plymouth, Conn.

W. BULL. **133 Rachael,**

Sire LIVING STORM 26; Dam FAWN 37; birth Feb'y 17th,
1869; bred by WM. BULL, Conn.

H. E. D.—J. G. **134 Butter Cup,**

Bred by ROSWELL L. COLT, Paterson, N. J., from his Import-
ed Stock; sold by JOHN GILES to H. E. DAY, at Connecticut
State Fair, at New Haven,—having taken first Premium in her
Class; J. A. TAINTOR being Chairman of Committee.

135 Brenda,

Imported by THOS. MOTLEY.

136 Duchess,

Imported by DAVID DANA, Lowell, Mass.

137 Daisy,

Prize Cow, imported by PARIAN STEVENS, Boston, Mass.; bred by L. GALLAIS, of La Moin, from first Prize Cow, by first Prize Bull, at Paris Exhibition.

138 Judy,

Sire COMET 116; Dam DAISY 137; birth 1860; bred by RANSOM REED, Lowell, Mass.; now owned by ASA BARTHOLOMEW, Bristol, Conn.

139 Lady Ashley. VI.

Color drab,—neck and ears French blue; birth 1867; from the herd of PHILIP NEEL, Ashley Court, St. John's Parish, Isle of Jersey; selected and imported by H. M. WELLINGTON, per Steamer Nestorian, and landed at Portland, Me., Jan. 29th, 1869; served on the Island of Jersey; owned by BURR S. BEACH, Terryville, Conn.

140 Lady Martin, XXVI.

Color dark drab,—a few white hairs in forehead,—black switch; birth 1867; from the herd of THOS. WM. MESSERVY, Fief de la Rien, St. Martins, Isle of Jersey; selected and imported by H. M. WELLINGTON, on Steamer Nestorian, and landed at Portland, Maine, Jan. 29th, 1869; served on the Island; now owned by S. R. GRIDLEY, Bristol, Conn.

141 Lola Montez, X.

Color dark fawn and some white; bug horns; birth 1867; selected and imported from the Isle of Jersey, by H. M. WELLINGTON, by Steamer Nestorian, at Portland, Jan. 29, 1869; served on the Island; now owned by S. R. GRIDLEY.

142 Lady Montague, L.

Color light fawn and white; bug horns; birth 1867; selected and imported from the Isle of Jersey, by H. M. WELLINGTON, per Steamer Austrian, to Portland, Feb., 1869; served on the Island; now owned by S. R. GRIDLEY, Bristol, Conn.

143 Lady Messervy, XXV,

Color dark drab,—star in forehead; birth 1867; from the herd of THOS. WM. MESSERVY, Fief de la Riene, St. Martins, Isle of Jersey; selected and imported by H. M. WELLINGTON, per Steamer Nestorian, to Portland, Jan'y 29, 1869; served on the Island to calve in June; now owned by WALLACE BARNES.

144 Lady Clarence, XVII.

Color light drab, buff, and some white,—star in forehead,— black in switch; bug horns; from the herd of CHAS. POIGNDES-TRE, No. 6 Clarence Terrace; selected and imported by H. M. WELLINGTON, per Steamer Nestorian, to Portland, Capt. DUT-TON, from Liverpool; landed Jan'y 29th, 1869; served on the Island; now owned by WALLACE BARNES, Bristol, Conn.

145 Amy, XII.

Color gray and white,—shield in forehead,—white switch; bug horns; from the herd of PHILIP AMY, Castillon de Bass Grouville, Isle de Jersey; birth April, 1867; selected and imported by H. M. WELLINGTON, per Steamer Nestorian, to Portland, Jan'y 29th, 1869; served on the Island; now owned by WALLACE BARNES.

146 Jessie,

Imported by TAINTOR & BUCK in 1851; owned by DANIEL BUCK, Poquonnock, Conn.

www.ingramcontent.com/pod-product-compliance
Lightning Source LLC
Chambersburg PA
CBHW021553270326
41931CB00009B/1200